FREE MY SON!

OBAMA'S POLITICALIZATION OF INTELLIGENCE AGENCIES FOR CRIMINAL ACTIVITIES

Artificial Intelligence (AI) Enslaves My Son's Brain

FREE MY SON!

A Father's Observation of Son's Seven Years Loss of Freedom and Liberty by the CIA

Andrew Jackson

**Will involuntary AI enslavement ever end?
When will it end?
How will it end?**

Fulton Books, Inc.
Meadville, PA

Published by Fulton Books 2020

ISBN 978-1-64654-669-5 (paperback)
ISBN 978-1-64654-670-1 (digital)

Printed in the United States of America

ACKNOWLEDGMENTS

A. To faith in the Great Triune God
   1. God the Holy Father in heaven
   2. God the Son Jesus Christ
   3. God the Holy Spirit
B. To my faithful wife of forty-four years
         No man could have a better woman as wife and mother of
   his only male child (only child)
C. To my brothers and sisters in Christ
   1. My pastor
   2. My Bible teacher
   3. Family radio (Oakland California)
   4. My son's Sunday school teachers and mentors (some of
      whom are named)
D. To my typist
E. To my sister and brother-in-law
F. To my late wife's sister
G. My son
H. To the Boy Scouts of America
I. To the American Boy Choir School
J. To Michael F. Bell—author of *The Invisible Crime*

CONTENTS

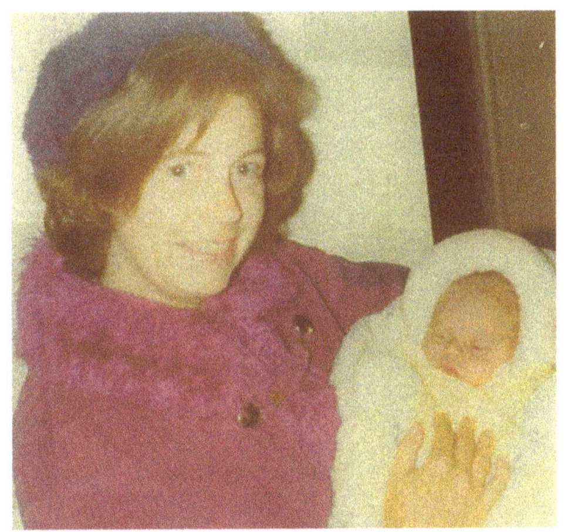

In the beginning
with Mom

Hanging out with
Mom and Dad

Hanging out with
Mom's Mom and Dad

A
Father's
Observations
of
His Son's
Involuntary
Confrontation
with
AI

Will it ever
end? If yes, when
will it end?
Are other
Americans
facing this
Involuntary AI enslavement?
How is it damaging
AI Enslavement's
participants
How are AI
participants
coping?

Hanging out with Mom's mom and dad (center) and some uncles, aunts and lots of cousins

My grandad
could get me
airborne!
Great fun!

Grandmom
does a
lot of
kissing!

Swimming
with
Dad

Beach fun

Having fun with the gang

Having fun alone

Exploring fun

Mom and I meet a very famous author of children's books.

My cowboy hat doesn't show up, but I am wearing one!

This pony horse is just my size!

If a pony horse is not around, there is always Dad!

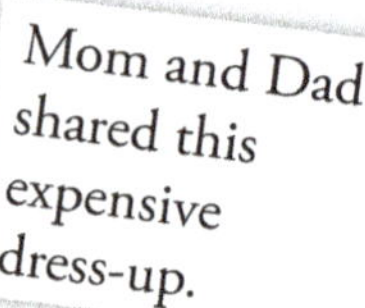

Mom and Dad shared this expensive dress-up.

Dressing up for school with Mom

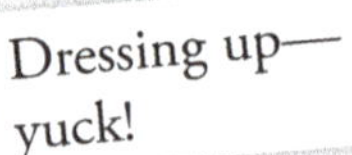

Dressing up—yuck!

DRESSING UP FOR MY EAGLE SCOUT
COURT OF HONOR

Dad's Family

Ancient family photos

At left: Nanny's dad—a genius who built a huge telescope!

At right: My dad's dad who passed away two years before I was born. My great-grandad and Mom are at left. That is *not* me in front. Guess who?

ABUSES OF ARTIFICIAL INTELLIGENCE: AI

Russian President Putin has stated on the internet that "whoever controls AI can control the world." Perhaps President Putin has been aware of the rapid transition of the Soviet Union, now Russia, from an agriculture to the industrial age as well as the transition from the industrial economy to the information age. President Putin is aware that the next transition, now underway, is the information economy to artificial intelligence.

What are examples of artificial intelligence? Robots, such as R2D2, made their first mass appearance in America with science fiction films. Military uses of robots' transition from rockets to pilot less drones.

Organized crime has been utilizing the insertion of microchips into the human body for the purpose of exploiting its victims in a great variety of ways. Author Michael F. Bell refers to this form of artificial intelligence as "the invisible crime." Bell's personal experience with illegal microchip implants—once discovered, they are extremely painful to surgically remove with persistent pain even after removal. Bell discovered through personal experience that the discovery and removal was not only difficult but extremely costly. Bell had to travel outside of the United States for detection of microchip implants illegally placed in his body by organized crime.

Humanity owes much to Michael F. Bell not only illegal microchip technology but also for microwave technology and its use against mankind in his true story in his book *The Invisible Crime*. This writer is deeply indebted to Bell not only for his courage and persistence in uncovering the dark side of AI. Thank you, again, Michael, for your well-written book!

My son has for about seven years endured microwave technology utilized illegally without his initial agreement. My admiration for my son reminds me of the courage of Michael F. Bell. For the first part of his microwave technology, my son endured this enslavement alone in his apartment. He was ordered by the voices in his head to leave his apartment and encouraged to sell his car. He complied and began living in hotels/motels with no human friendships. As his father, I could only see him briefly and only rarely did we share a meal together in a restaurant. As his father, my struggling son could only briefly text me that he was alive.

A parent's worst nightmare visited me when all contact with a son completely stopped. There were no more text messages. As I was unable to contact the police, which will be described later, I began a search by calling a Best Western hotel in the last area, which was the last location of contact. My telephone call to the first, and only hotel, yielded no positive results.

As a volunteer Christian chaplain, I began to pray to our Great Triune God.

The Lord's positive guidance was answered almost instantaneously for the early morning drive search led me to my son's hotel, one of many dozens in the area! Thank you, God!

After utilizing our secret knock on his room door, he opened the door appearing with a bandage on his face. The torment that my son from his AI experiment had caused him to fall; however, having earned an MD degree, he was able to bandage his wound so skillfully that he avoided going to obtain medical intervention. Based upon my son's experience with hospitals, emergency rooms, seeking medical intervention might result in his third involuntary admission to a mental facility. I was present when he was involuntarily admitted to such a facility. It was a setup for the AI experience he would need to endure for seven years which continues as of this writing.

I informed the medical officials that my son was never suicidal and that I would take full responsibility by staying with my son to monitor him. Not only did these medical authorities refuse my request, the medical facility charged him $13,000 over his Blue Cross Blue Shield insurance policy. In retrospect, a setup for AI experimentation was likely because he endured a MRI brain scan. After inquiring about the results of the brain scan, I was informed that the test was no cause for concern. I concluded that a setup for a long-term AI experiment was a decided possibility.

Returning to my reunion with my injured son at the last hotel residence, my son agreed to return home with me. Our residential home was the same single family dwelling in which he lived with my wife and me.

AI experimentation at a variety of hotel/motel rooms compared to AI experience at home. My son seemed to be more comfortable at home. His laughter was "music to my ears." He was cooperative and pleasant with his tormentors. On one of two meals that we were allowed together, I remarked to him that he might want to be less pleasant with the voices in his head because they were probably utilizing his answers to questions that they posed might possibly be needed for job training purposes. My son informed me that his tormentors told him to tell me that no, they were not involved in on-the-job training. For four years at our home, we were not allowed to share meals together anymore. Additionally, my son's acid torture and sleep deprivation continued.

LOSS OF LIBERTY AND FREEDOM!

My son's personal freedom was reduced to nearly nothing. He had to obtain permission to vote or obtain a haircut. AI is worse than the 1984 Big Brother image. AI is with you 100 percent of the time. My son, at least while living with me in his boyhood home, made the very best of "AI Big Brother." We both had to adjust to short "HI-BYE" discussions as we were not allowed to converse at any length. For example, I requested a brief ten-minute "time-out" to celebrate my son's birthday. He agreed and he paid the price from AI with a session of nausea. Our brief birthday celebration had to be cancelled. His ongoing torture was most often limited to acid torture and sleep deprivation. Additionally, he was required to spend most of his daylight hours in our screened-in back porch with the sliding back door closed in order that I could not observe my son's conversations with the evil AI.

Why would any father put up and even tolerate such an arrangement? For both of us, it was much more preferred than a son living at great length in a hotel/motel room. To deal with my guilt, I wrote many letters to elected and/or recently appointed officials in the federal government for relief. The political turbulence of the very first few months of the new Trump administration resulted in no reply(ies). Finally, my persistence resulted in a very long telephone conversation with a representative from the United States Veterans Administration. After pouring out my heart and soul to a very kind and empathetic VA rep, who was also a single parent who became aware that I was a widower, further positive action was hopeful. Our case was to be transferred from the VA Administration to the US Justice Department.

Why did I refuse to notify the law enforcement officials on a local or state level? Fear precluded me to do so because after observing my son "talking to himself" it would result in another needless trip to a mental institution.

Fear manipulation motivated both father and son. My son had infinitely more courage that the father. The son had no one to confide in other than Almighty God. I prayed that he would avail his suffering to Almighty God. The prayers of mine to our Great Triune God (God the Father in Heaven, God the Son—Jesus Christ and God—the Holy Spirit) kept my sanity activated most of the time. As a weak human being, I confess to periods of anger in front of my son. My son, very rarely, displayed any sign of anger. He was convinced that he was helping AI fight crime and sending criminals to prison.

As a father, I could confide in my pastor, my family, my brothers and sisters in Christ, and most importantly, my prayers to Almighty God in the name of His Son, Jesus Christ, a source I prayed that my son was also relying upon. Again and again, God answered my prayers to balance a weak earthly father and my son, who demonstrated great strength for both father and son.

Did my son have another source of real or non-real strength? In retrospect, I think he put too much hope on a "unwritten DEAL" with AI. He assured me that he was not guilty of any crime, so I assumed that the DEAL might refer to a financial settlement as my son had no opportunity to have employment or even to drive a car. He had faith and hope in the protection of AI. In contrast, I had little. My son had a focus on locks and security (ADT). When I failed to lock one of three locks on our door, it resulted in a rare falling out between father and son. Nevertheless, our strange situation was one of mutual love and support. Without speaking, we both did actions to not only support each other but demonstrated love, which spoke louder than words.

In the final analysis of father-son relationships, I was supported by our Great Triune God, as well as my son's laughter with

AI in the rare times I could hear a one-sided conversation with AI. Additionally, I had no doubt that my son had no mental problems with the exception of some obsessive compulsive behavior. He had never experienced entertainment drugs; however, his reliance on over-the-counter pain medications and a need to consume large amounts of baking soda to deal with his AI acid torture did give me causes for concern.

A lack of human face-to-face relationships during the four years at our home, together with about three years in his apartment and countless hotels/motels there were no meaningful human relationships with friends, relatives or even strangers. He was ordered by AI not to talk with others at all times. If he spoke to me at any length, he paid the price with either acid torture or nausea. Additionally, he was ordered not to watch TV or listen to radio. He was allowed to carry a cell phone and order personal needs from Amazon. This somewhat isolated existence must have had some purpose(s). Was my son being screened for a one-way trip to Mars?

MY SON'S RESUME

As a young boy, Sesame Street ignited a love of learning together with reading.

My late wife and I requested and received permission from our local public school district for our son's advanced grade placement. However, the request and permission to meet our son's educational needs were unexpectantly cancelled. For this reason, our son is the product of excellent private school education. He was the poor boy in classes of privileged students. For example, we learned from our son that our rewards for his achievement were pennies compared to dollars from the parents of his classmates. It made little difference to our son as he loved learning.

He entered postsecondary education at an advanced placement and was younger than most of his college classmates. He was offered the opportunity to attempt original cancer and AIDs research at the National Cancer Institute at Fort Detrick, Maryland. His supervisor, Dr. David Hodge, encouraged our son in many ways. David and his wife and my late wife and I became friends. At the conclusion of our son's period with David, he received an unusual surprise. It was a standard practice at that time for the supervisor of underlings to accept credit for any significant accomplishment of their young charges. The practice was justified because of the time invested by the supervisor toward his/her charges. Dr. Hodge changed this practice with our son's original research by placing our son's name on his research. Dr. Hodge indicated that our son had accomplished research that Dr. Hodge would have undertaken if his time and focus had permitted.

The kind action of Dr. David Hodge made it possible for our son to enter a prestigious graduate school with no charges whatever together with a stipend. He received his master of science in pathology. He applied to medical school, just one, and was immediately accepted. He received his MD degree.

Before proceeding to his life after obtaining the MD degree, I would like to include what my late wife and I would consider factors which led to our son's academic success. During his expensive K-12 private education, my late wife and I tried to keep other activities and interests in our young son's life. My late wife and I were soccer parents, Tiger Cub Scout leaders, and Boy Scout parents on an exceptional troop. Our son loved the Boy Scouts and earned almost all of the merit badges the Boy Scouts offered. Our son returned his teaching skills to younger Scouts by teaching a variety of merit badges. I had the opportunity on many occasions to observe his teaching of some of the merit badges together with Scout masters and assistant Scout masters. His "payback" to the Boy Scouts was appreciated. Our son valued his rank of Eagle Scout and included it on his résumé.

Our son was blessed by our Great Triune God with both Methodist and Presbyterian Churches and their respective Sunday school teachers, including, but not limited to, Mary Taylor Jenkins and Joseph Ross. Victor Rosso was his mentor in earning the God and Country Merit Badge.

After graduating from medical school, he searched for placement with minimal requirements for attending pregnant mothers with delivering babies. Either our son's research in this direction was inadequate or the medical residency he selected changed their policy, our son delivered many more babies than he had expected. All babies delivered by our son were without incident which is regarded as successful.

After completing his residency, the next career move was the acceptance of a medical director in a correctional facility. When my late wife was in the last stage of her battle with cancer, our son took a family leave to assist my wife and me with hospice care. At about this time, our son was hit with another crisis. He was named in litigation regarding the death of a four-week old baby in the facility where he served his medical residency. It was a shock to us because our son did not deliver the baby, he did not attend the baby and was not responsible for those attending the baby.

My wife on her death bed informed our son that we would front load a large legacy to him if he would not practice medicine and consider returning to medical research and/or teaching medicine. He agreed and resigned his position as medical director. After my wife's passing, our son's life was troubled with this ongoing court case regarding the death of a four-week baby. Litigation continued for months and months turned into years. While he had no involvement with the death of the baby, it was extremely disruptive on a personal and career basis.

No sooner was he absolved from the baby court case, he was notified of new litigation while serving as the medical director in the correctional facility. The legal advice he received was good news as there was no basis for the new legal issues. While this was good news it resulted in a joint decision between my son and me to delay the transfer of some of my property to my son. With the assistance of my late wife's sister, my son and myself we required considerable time in disposing of our second residence in a housing market that collapsed as a result of subprime mortgage crisis. Week after week and month after month, we worked together to dispose of household belongings while other homes in our neighborhood remained in foreclosure. During this time, my son and I relied on each other and our bond had never been stronger.

After selling the house, we agreed that my son would reside in a new complex and I would return to another home (our son's boyhood home) in a different state. I invited my son to return home with me to conserve his financial resources. He declined at this point in time but accepted a few years later.

ADVANTAGES OF AI?

Artificial intelligence, if humanely utilized, can help us focus issues considered important by *benevolent* users. It can be an excellent tool for investigative efforts.

Do we, as a nation, need to keep up with Russia's Putin? Perhaps until the second coming of Jesus Christ, many humans will be motivated to engage in criminal enterprises.

Persons who engage in crime are very often highly intelligent. Nations who are, or could be, enemies of America maintain intelligence agencies. America seems to rely *heavily* on intelligence agencies.

Was the competition between the CIA and the FBI responsible in any way for a failure to prevent the attack on the New York World Trade Center Towers in 2001 (as well as other adjacent buildings)? Was there a need to establish the NSA after 9/11?

Was the Patriot Act after 9/11 responsible for preventing future attacks on America? Only time will tell when the public may or may not receive "the truth" under the Freedom of Information Act. Will the intelligence agencies be able to reveal the advantage(s) of AI under the Freedom of Information Act which could be of value to enemies or potential enemies of America? Could revelations of AI be used, for good or evil, in legal cases affecting court rulings?

In the final analysis of the advantage(s) of AI, will AI gain new intelligence on how new criminal practices are and how being deployed and dealing with a complete loss of freedom and privacy. Apparently, AI has the ability to understand even private thoughts (and secrets) never articulated!

After living with my son for four years, I am conflicted as whether or not the CIA is playing Almighty God. From time to time,

I hear my son laughing and seemingly enjoying his conservation(s) which can occur anytime 24-7. My son is always separated from me, so I rarely hear this laughter. Conversely, I can tell when he is subject to torture (acid torture, nausea, and/or sleep deprivation).

One of my great concerns regarding the long-term effect(s) the microwave voice-to-skull technology will have on his brain. Will my son have a brain tumor and if so, will it be cancerous? Is my son undergoing an AI experiment (among other purposes) on his brain? For example, after one of his trips to the emergency room visits, he underwent an MRI scan of his brain. As my son's medical advocate, I discovered that the MRI brain scan was acceptable for a male of his age. Will my son be subjected to another MRI brain scan at the end of his involuntary enslavement? Will my son's enslavement ever end? Will my son be healthy at the end (if there is an end) of his enslavement?

If AI was utilized in any matter in gathering CIA intelligence to avoid the attack destruction of a church in St. Petersburg, Russia, then it was a significant advantage! Russian president Putin extended his appreciation to President Trump for sharing this CIA intelligence. As a result, radical Islamic terrorists did not succeed and their plans were foiled.

The Russian's helped defeat Hitler's Third Reich in World War II. Without Russian-American partnership with the building and upkeep/provisioning of the International Space Station, this enterprise might not have succeeded or at least maintained after its construction.

DISADVANTAGES OF AI

AI takes a toll on persons who are targets of CIA, FBI, and NSA. If guilt is clearly a near absolute and the intelligence agencies need to uncover a wide or wider scope and view of criminal practice(s) the use of AI may be needed. Additionally, if an enemy, or potential enemy, AI may be needed.

From my observations of my son over the past seven years (and especially over the past four years while living with me), AI practices appear to be overly controlling of his US Constitutional rights. To my knowledge, my son was never charged with any crime. He seems to be in some sort of DEAL (unwritten) with the CIA. My son informed me that he *committed* no crime. He would not (or could not) expand on the terms of this unwritten DEAL. I, as a father, trust my son regarding not being a criminal and his willingness to assist the CIA in its fight of crime. Will my son receive financial compensation of, to date, about seven years taken out of his life and dealing with a complete loss of freedom and privacy? Apparently, AI has the ability to understand even private thoughts (and secrets) never articulated!

After living with my son for four years, I am conflicted as whether or not the CIA is playing Almighty God. From time to time, I hear my son laughing and seemingly enjoying his conversation(s) which can occur anytime 24-7. My son is always separated from me, so I rarely hear this laughter. Conversely, I can tell when he is subject to torture (acid torture, nausea and /or sleep deprivation).

One of my great concerns regarding the long-term effect(s) the microwave voice-to-skull technology will have on his brain. Will my son have a brain tumor and if so, will it be cancerous? Is my son undergoing an AI experiment (among other purposes) on his brain?

Once again, after one of his trips to the Emergency Room, he underwent an MRI scan of his brain. As my son's medical advocate, I discovered that the MRI brain scan was acceptable for a male of his age. Will my son be subjected to another MRI brain scan at the end of his involuntary enslavement? Will my son's enslavement ever end? Will my son be healthy at the end (if there is an end) of his enslavement?

As a father of a great son, what can I do to assist my son? Do I trust the military who according to my son is responsible for his torture to assure his cooperation with the CIA?

Even though the first year of the Trump Administration was a *turbulent* period in American history, I have reached out to the Veteran's Administration and they responded with a long conversation with me. The VA representative was assuring and promised to forward our case to the US Justice Department. Thank you, God!

In summary, I realize that my son is completely sane and always has been sane in spite of two trips to a mental institution! It is possible that the medical community might have colluded with the CIA for his selection for the AI enslavement period. Apparently, Miranda rights do not need to be presented to mentally ill patients. The other possibility would be the inability of the mental institutions to have patients with excellent medical insurance. My son was billed $13,000 over his insurance coverage. Perhaps this cost which exceeded his medical coverage was needed to provide suicidal watch while in the hospital dealing with his physical recovery. My objections on his last hospitalization were to no avail. My son has never used any drugs "for entertainment purposes." He never has abused alcohol in my presence drinking one glass of wine at most.

During my son's AI enslavement, he has had to rely on over-the-counter pain medication on an ongoing process. He has paid his dues to his country! Please stop CIA (and military if involved) killing my son. I rely on Almighty God's willingness to make the CIA (and military) fully aware of the harm inflicted over the past seven years. You have not allowed me any father-son conversations other than HI-BYE type exchanges. I pray that my son's continual cooperation will in some way benefit America. Nevertheless, enough is enough.

May my son's involuntary AI enslavement end soon! Will his AI enslavement ever end? When will my son's involuntary AI enslavement end? How will AI enslavement end? Will my son have a blessed future after AI enslavement? Praise God—"all things work together for good who trust in Him and who are called according to his purposes!"

A FATHER'S APPRECIATION TO A SON WHO DISPLAYED COURAGE AND LOVE OF HIS COUNTRY AND ITS CONSTITUTION AND THE FREEDOM IT AFFORDS

1. May you regain after AI the full measure of freedom and liberty soon and in good health!
2. I love you, and you know your mom loves you looking down at you from heaven!
3. Only the trust and love of our Great Triune God could have challenged my patience with your unwelcomed challenge with AI!
4. I pray that your trust and love in our Great Triune God will get you through your unusual challenge with AI!
5. I trust your future on earth and in heaven will be happier and joyful!
6. I trust you will never stop relying on your Holy Father in heaven, your Savior Jesus Christ, and the indwelling Holy Spirit in the likely event I will pass from this earth before your challenge with AI is not concluded! I love you, son!

I VOLUNTEERED! MY SON WAS INVOLUNTARILY ENSLAVED!

Photo taken by my late-wife when we were both twenty-one and unmarried at this point in time. My son and I still love America, which is still the best country in the world with all its faults. My son's love of country must be much stronger than mine because of his endurance with illegal sonic voice-to-skull technology (utilizing microwave technology)!

In my day, the military had thirty days of paid liberty or leave when you were free to travel to home or friends. For at least four years, and probably seven years, my son has had no leave or liberty to travel. He must get permission for me to take him for haircuts during which time we must not talk to each other!

My son was involuntary enslaved in the CIA with AI voices subjecting his brain 24-7 with interrupted sleep. He made an unwritten DEAL with the CIA with an undetermined end (if there is an end). My son is a true patriot, even if he was drafted into a DEAL WITH THE DEVIL!

MESSAGE FROM A CONCERNED DAD TO THE CIA: WHEN IS ENOUGH ENOUGH? Is enough when he has a brain tumor or when he is dead?

The CIA has possibly been manipulating my son with the "good cop/bad cop" routine. For example, he indicated that the CIA was not responsible for his enslavement, but rather the military. Further, he was informed that he was not safe in his apartment and was apparently told to leave. He did.

My son's car was sold because apparently you can't concentrate with driving and undergo CIA interrogation at the same time.

Will the CIA terminate my son's service to the nation by allowing him to enter a mental institution in order to extract additional years of experimental torture? Will my son be either conscripted into the service of the CIA or an unwilling candidate for participating in the establishment of a planet Mars colony? What is his indoctrination or experimentation all about?

Any member of the military knows, from the beginning of service, the termination date in the future. Reenlistment is purely voluntary.

Does the Patriot Act (post-9/11) have the power to involuntarily enlist an American for loss of liberty and freedom? Was the FISA court involved with this loss of liberty and freedom? Are participants indoctrinated to believe that they were voluntarily or involuntarily involved in a criminal activity? Is this another possible tool utilized by the CIA for control?

In any event, it appears that CIA involuntary participants may be in an involuntary NO WIN SITUATION! I certainly hope not! If an unwritten CIA DEAL extends for a lifetime, isn't such a DEAL totally worthless?

AN OLD FATHER'S EFFORT TO FIGHT POLITICAL CORRECTNESS WHICH HAD THE POTENTIAL TO HELP BOTH MY COUNTRY AND MY SON

The following OP/ED (without my name) was sent to over fifty "Letters to the Editor" and or editor primarily in battleground states in the mid-2016.

I have no way of monitoring the publication results but the effort was worth the fight to diminish political correctness if only one Midwestern editor published an old man's OP/ED. In mid-2016, I felt a new birth of freedom and liberty dawning which in some way might help my son's involuntary enslavement with an artificial intelligence experiment which reminded me of Project Mockingbird!!

COVER LETTER FOR MY OP/ED DURING THE 2016 PRESIDENTIAL ELECTION

Dear Editor:

Enclosed please find my OP/ED entitled "A Vote for Trump Affirms Women's Rights"

The reason for my partial identity is a result of a crime mob known as the "Black Muslims." I do not want to have my family targeted.

My OP/ED has publication potential in the following:

1. Election of 2016 / Presidential Debates
2. Women's Issues
3. The Dangers of Political Correctness
4. Contrast Between the World's Two Largest Religions

Thank you for your consideration.

Sincerely,
A U.S. Navy Veteran

Enclosure

A VOTE FOR TRUMP AFFIRMS WOMEN'S RIGHTS

The firm stand Donald J. Trump has taken early in the Republican Primary process for identifying the Radical Islamic threat to America greatly affirms the rights of women! Trump recognized that the "political correctness" employed by President Barack Obama and former Secretary of State Hillary Clinton over nearly eight years, has given aid and comfort to not only the Radical Islam but also to all Muslims who strongly believe in the centuries-old Sharia law which has kept its women in a distant second-class and brutally repressive condition since the founding of the world's largest religion.

The founder of the world's second largest religion, Jesus Christ, affirmed the rights and importance of women many centuries before Islam. Two thousand years' ago, Jesus Christ observed a mob of men about to stone a known adulteress to death. Jesus approached the men and said "he who is without sin may cast the first stone." Slowly, and one-by-one, the men left the potential death scene until only the adulteress and Jesus remained. Jesus turned to the woman and said, "They do not condemn you and neither do I, but go and sin no more."

If Judeo-Christian values are to survive together with Western Civilization it is essential that the truth, without spin, must prevail over political correctness throughout the Western and freedom-loving nations. Trump has demonstrated that identifying Radical Islam as America's enemy was the first step in addressing the failure of America with the confrontation with its enemy. Trump has also proposed possible solutions which have the potential of addressing this severe threat to America much more effectively than the past eight years of President Obama and former Secretary of State Hillary Clinton.

A vote for Hillary Clinton, in spite of her gender, will assure the decline of the political, economic and social rights of both genders with the continued pursuit of the failed policy of political correctness.

A vote for Donald Trump will begin to stop the hemorrhaging of America's strength at home and abroad for not only both genders but also for all of the many races of legal citizens. In time, America will grow stronger and even to assume its position of leader of the free-world at a time when the European Union is faltering.

Respectively submitted
by an honorable
discharged active duty
U.S. Navy Vet.

A TRIBUTE TO PRESIDENT DONALD J TRUMP

Thank you, Mr. President Trump, for the modern-day presidential fireside chats known as Tweets! Keep them coming! The left has few, if any, moderates and too many legislative votes demonstrate with zero votes. The Democrats (not members of the Democratic Party) are no longer independent Democratic voters. Additionally, after your highly presidential first-year accomplishments, the Democrats and the mainstream print and electronic media are still not over your Electoral College landslide victory in the 2016 presidential election! The paid rioters on your inauguration day damaging property and vehicles was truly un-American. They were *not* protesters, which is always acceptable in America, but anarchists who were apparently highly paid for their despicable violence! Members of the Democrat Party and the liberal mainstream media apparently were strangely quiet and seemingly void of any condemnation. Nevertheless, it was a day of a very important transfer of power under the US Constitution.

Mr. President, you received a grade of A+ from your supporters for almost superhuman effort and for the many significant accomplishments in your first year! Many Americans are totally unaware of your highly successful diplomatic achievements during your first-year Asian trip. Please continue to Tweet your many accomplishments otherwise even your supporters will not always be able to fully appreciate them. You are not going to be charged with boasting or braying. No president can possibly meet the liberal standards of "presidential" when they are simultaneously plotting your impeachment!

America needs seven more years of President Donald J. Trump followed by another eight years of your faithful and loyal vice president Mike Pence! I hope Mr. Pence has the insight to follow through with your policies and direction.

Why would an elderly father who is deeply concerned about a son's loss of freedom and liberty be so supportive of your continued success in so many areas? You are truly an advocate of both genders and all racial groups who love America!

I pray for a rebirth of freedom and liberty for all Americans of all races and socioeconomic classes. Perhaps my son will regain his freedom and liberty without his father's need to request a presidential pardon. Until such a request is forthcoming, I provide priorities and needs that you are fully aware and of which you are supportive. Following are such needs are listed:

1. Keep tweeting! In an age of an absence of real news, half-truths and outright fake news (propaganda), all Americans need to know your thoughts, your stand on all issues and your accomplishments.
2. Be ever mindful that the Republicans are not aware of "circling the wagons" on any issue. Please be patient with them in this important transition to a more rational approach for America. With few exceptions Democrats range from Socialist to Communist in their approach to most issues. Republicans must not want any love from Democrats or expect any light from them.
3. Continue to return to hardworking Americans as much of their earnings as possible while showing as much of the nation's resources to those in need as possible (victims of storms, etc.).
4. Harden the electrical grid which was a plank on the Republican Party platform. The Democrats have never afforded this issue any importance whatsoever. America, and any nation, could be completely devastated if the elec-

trical grid goes down due to solar flares, sabotage, storms, and one region's failure, causing another region's grid failure.

5. Revise or cancel the Civil Service status of all Federal employees granted by former president Obama.

6. Watch your back, Mr. Trump. Presidential security is needed but not totally adequate. Until America becomes more transformed to a more civil community, please consider maintaining your loyal privately employed body guards. Former president John F. Kennedy is "talking to you" from the grave.

7. Know that so many love you, Mr. President. It cannot be taken away. Nevertheless, please keep tweeting! We need to know your reports, your successes, what still needs to be accomplished. You have every right to display your frustration from time to time. Your supporters were also very frustrated prior to your landslide election. Thank you, Mr. President!

8. May our Great Triune God richly bless you, President Trump, your family, the vice president, the three branches of the Federal government, and their respective families and staffs! God bless you all and God bless America until the second coming of Jesus Christ!

With best wishes

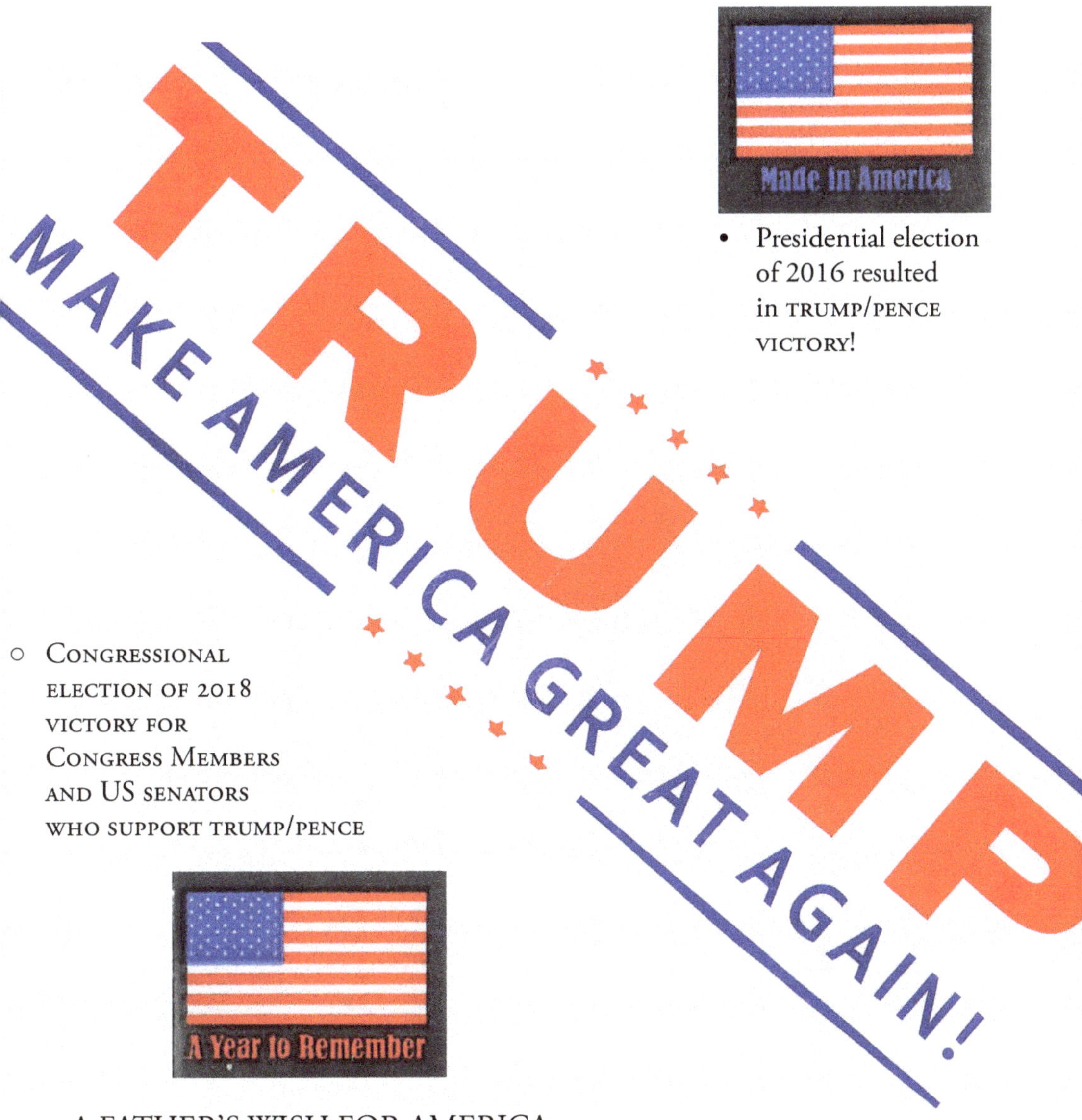

- Presidential election of 2016 resulted in TRUMP/PENCE VICTORY!

○ CONGRESSIONAL ELECTION OF 2018 VICTORY FOR CONGRESS MEMBERS AND US SENATORS WHO SUPPORT TRUMP/PENCE

A FATHER'S WISH FOR AMERICA

○ Congressional election of 2022 VICTORY for members of Congress who support TRUMP/PENCE

- Presidential election 2020 result in overwhelming victory for TRUMP/PENCE

Since mid-2016 Dad has been a "proud deplorable" and an ardent supporter of President Trump. The president had no traditional honeymoon immediately after the 2016 presidential election because Mr. Trump's victory was not "decreed" by the self-appointed printed press and electronic media and their shock that they do not control the American people! Instead of embracing America's will, the press/electronic media responded with unprecedented hate campaign. President Trump's extraordinary accomplishments result in another productive second term! Godspeed Mr. Trump and please FREE MY SON! Thank You!

EPILOGUE

1. Will my son continue for a lifetime of CIA enslavement, because of AI, and truly have privacy, freedom and liberty?
2. Will AI's sonic microwave sonic voice-to-skull technology return even if ever granted a presidential pardon?
3. What damage to the US Constitution has been caused by AI in the past years, present and future years?
4. Since 9/11 and the attacks on New York City and Washington, DC, have there been self-imposed losses of freedom and liberty provided by the Patriot Act enacted after 9/11?
5. Will the son ever look at his father and interact with detailed conversations with him, without being reminded of the nausea, acid torture and sleep deprivation on the rare times the son has (or wanted) to reach out to his Dad during his AI experience?
6. To what extent was his Christian and family experiences an assistance to keep him sane from day after day, week after week, month after month, and year after year?
7. What brain damage, if any, was inflicted by AI even if AI were immediately terminated?
8. With daily possibilities to provide true or false future possible criminal charges to my son because of AI?
9. Will my son be able to trust anyone anymore because of his AI abuse, lack of privacy, loss of freedom, and liberty?
10. Will my son be able to have any faith of the unwritten terms of the DEAL he believes he has with the CIA?
11. Will my son be able to put the AI experience behind him and return to his faith and/or strengthen his faith in our Great Triune God?

12. Was the FISA court inappropriately and/or politically motivated in my son's selection for AI enslavement for seven years with dangerous sonic microwave voice-to-skull technology?

13. In the Korean War in the 1950s, American and Allied captured troops were not allowed to reply to their captors with just Geneva Convention rules to only reveal their name, rank and serial number. Instead, they were also subjected to intense "braining washing"/indoctrination. It is understandable that some captured troops (because of torture and intense indoctrination) agreed with their captors to the point of degrading the United States of America.

IMPORTANT QUESTION

Has the AI/sonic microwave voice-to-skull technology adversely affected my son after seven years of intensive 24-7 (6:00 AM or earlier to midnight or later) interrogation? My son is exceptionally strong mentally; however, the past seven years has taken a toll on him!

As a father of a great son, what can I do to assist my son? Do I trust the military who according to my son is responsible for his torture to assure his cooperation with the CIA?

Even though the first year of the Trump Administration was a *turbulent* period in American history, I have reached out to the Veterans Administration, and they responded with a long conversation with me. The VA representative was assuring and promised to forward our case to the US Justice Department. Thank you, God!

In summary, I realize that my son is completely sane, and always has been sane in spite of two trips to a mental institution. It is possible that the medical community might have colluded with the CIA for his selection for the AI enslavement period. Apparently, Miranda rights do not need to be presented to mentally ill patients. The other possibility would be the inability of the mental institutions to have patients with excellent medical insurance. My son was billed $13,000 over his insurance coverage. Perhaps this cost which exceeded his medical coverage was needed to provide suicidal watch while in the hospital dealing with his physical recovery. My objections on his last hospitalization were to no avail. My son has never used any drugs "for entertainment purposes." He never has abused alcohol in my presence drinking one glass of wine at most.

During my son's AI enslavement, he has had to rely on over-the-counter pain medication on an ongoing process. He has paid his dues to his country! Please stop CIA (and military if involved) killing my son. I rely Almighty God's willingness to make the CIA (and military) fully aware of this harm inflicted over the past seven years. You have not allowed me any father-son conversations other than HI-BYE type exchanges. I pray that my son's continual cooperation will in some way benefit America. Nevertheless, enough is enough.

May my son's involuntary AI enslavement end soon! Will his AI enslavement ever end? When will my son's involuntary AI enslavement end? How will AI enslavement end? Will my son have a blessed future after AI enslavement? Praise God—"all things work together for good who trust in Him and who are called according to His purpose!"

APPENDIX A

OTHER OBSERVATIONS BY AN ANGRY GOP DAD
FOR THE DISASTER OF 8 YEARS OF FORMER
PRESIDENT OBAMA AND THE DEMOCRAT
(NOT DEMOCRATIC) PARTY (2008–2016)

In addition to the expanded Patriot Act of the Obama Administration to enslave my son, the following include, but are not limited, to our more than two centuries of the unique American political and social experiment:

- Socialism and/or Communism
- Obamacare with soaring Healthcare premiums
- Politicization of the IRS, FBI, CIA, NSA, DOJ
- Illegal immigration for NEW DEMOCRAT VOTES
- Loss of Journalism with the same narratives repeated over and over instead of investigation
- Staged public protests resulting in violence
- Economic stagnation
- Slowed significant NASA progress
- Doubled the National Debt
- No progress on voter ID
- Weaker U.S. Military
- Weaken public communication with Political Correctness
- No progress in race relations, instead regression
- Encouraged Anti-Jewish sentiment in America and Israel
- Strengthened Iran with inadequate verification of a nuclear weapons state

- Illegal influence in the elections of Israel and America
- Disregard for the U.S. Constitution and the rule of law
- Corruption of the FISA courts probably enslaving my son
- Disrespect of law enforcement officials
- Used Patriot Act to promote an era of Big Brother watching peace-abiding citizens
- Favored Islam over Christianity and Judaism
- Lacked a work ethic while President
- Divided American citizens
- Promoted Globalism over National Security and Interests
- What Americans were hopeful in the Presidential Elections of 2008 and 2012 is not what America received
- Loss of progress of Affirmative Action Programs
- Encouraged propaganda views instead of truth in news
- Inadequate description of the Benghazi defeat in Libya
- Promoted Abortion with public funds to Planned Parenthood. Since 1973 over 50 million recorded abortions have been performed with a disproportional number of African-American babies lost. Many Christian children are taught the Sunday School song that "Jesus loves the little children all the children of the world red or yellow black or white they are precious in his sight." Jesus said that anyone who harms his little ones is in <u>deep, deep</u> trouble! Please take note. Planned Parenthood and its supporters!
- Failure to understand the need to harden the nation's electrical grid system for many reasons (storms, sabotage, solar flares, hacking, etc.)
- Failure to partner with American corporations
- Promoted the destruction of gender identity
- Failure to identify the danger of Radical Islam to American and Western societies on the planet
- Failure to recognize the uniqueness of America
- Excessive apologizing for America's faults and shortcomings
- Failure to promote the progress of American values to promote freedom and liberty for all citizens

- The migration of senior citizens living and working in blue states and needing to retire in red states with fiscal responsibility and lower state taxes. Fiscally responsible red states are punished by blue state retirees

May our Great Triune God continue to have mercy, grace and blessings on our beloved America. <u>GODSPEED</u> to President Trump and Vice President Pence in the Congressional Election of 2018, the Presidential Election of 2020 and the Congressional Election of 2022 (as well as the following GOP successors). It will take a long time to right the SHIP OF STATE!!!

APPENDIX B

GOP IS GFG

The GOP is (and has been) Government for Grownups!

Historically, the two party system has served America well. Each party has, thus far, served to provide a check on the political influence and power of the other party. This period in American history was characterized by moderates in each party. The moderates in each party not only kept the campaign discourse civil but they also provided a type of communication that could eventually lead to grudgingly accepted compromise for each political party.

The Presidential Election of 2016 marked the official end of America's ideal two-party system with the Democrat Presidential Candidate attacking the supporters of the GOP with the description of "deplorable" for supporters of the GOP standard-bearer.

The events following the election of Donald J Trump to the Office of President (who won by a landslide in the Electoral College) was barely a peaceful transfer of power from a corrupt administration to a new one. For example, Inauguration Day was marked with protestors and paid domestic terrorists setting fire to vehicles and smashing windows. All Americans have the right to peacefully conduct protest marches but <u>not to</u> accept riots!

Undoubtedly, there are still American Socialist/Communists who do not believe in the peaceful transfer of power after the

American people have spoken. The efforts to degrade a highly successful first-year of the Trump Administration demonstrated a wide variety of immature efforts to damage a successful President Trump (who never had a traditional "honeymoon period"). When the Russian connection charges failed, charges of insanity followed. To the credit of President Trump, the Presidential reply was stability as a genius in leading a divided GOP party to pass a tax reduction plan without a single Democrat vote of support in the U.S. Senate. Rather than embracing success for America gained by the GOP, is the Democrat Party (not Democratic Party) becoming increasingly irrational by refusing to move away from an obstructionist position to one of moderation through compromise. Will the Democrats continue to adopt the position of "our way or the highway"?

WILL OUR NATION'S LIGHT BE EXTINGUISHED?

The Socialist Democrat Party has engaged in a coup to overthrow the duly elected President Donald J. Trump. Additionally, the Socialist-Democrats have obstructed issues related to our nation's well-being with its priority of obtaining political power.

In spite of on-going attempts of coup and impeachment efforts, President Trump has had extraordinary accomplishments fulfilling campaign promises. Therefore, President Trump and many Republicans deserve our vote.

Why does Trump and most Republicans deserve our vote? Trump and most Republicans want the Great American Experiment to continue for our children and grandchildren. Early in our history as a nation we stood up to a powerful England and the Barbary Pirates in the Mediterranean Sea. Our nation's constitution and its Bill of Rights are the envy of many Socialist Democrats. Republican President Abraham Lincoln's Emancipation in 1863 started a long path toward equality for African-American and the subsequent Reconstruction was not fulfilled largely in part of Lincoln's assassination after the Civil War.

Please consider voting for Trump and Republican.

———

CULTURAL WAR AND/ OR THE SECOND US CIVIL WAR 2016–?

The success of President Donald Trump is not responsible for either a cultural war or what may be described as a non-shooting Second U.S. Civil War. President Trump's accomplishments during his first two years in office was marked by reduction of individual taxes, reduction of regulation and now trade deals with friends and potential foes. The radical left opposed President Trump at every opportunity. The president demonstrated great patience with the "witch hunt" by the independent council who investigated the wrong political party under Hillary Clinton who did have shameful dealings with Russia both before and after the Presidential Election of 2016.

President Trump also had to also cope with the liberal print and electronic media's propaganda on a daily basis. The Democrat Party has proudly adopted the socialist label.

Additionally, the Obama Administration's huge number of U.S. Circuit Judges and appointments to the DOJ, FBI, CIA AND NASA politicized and weaponized presented more challenges for President Trump who fulfilled his campaign promises. The President's extraordinary accomplishments under such unfair opposition is truly remarkable!

President Donald J. Trump truly deserves a second term as he can avoid a cultural war and a second U.S. Civil War. Vote Republican.

Enclosure #1

THE WHITE HOUSE

WASHINGTON

May 16, 2019

Thank you for taking the time to write to me. Your kind words and steadfast support mean a great deal.

Every day, I am working to uphold the values we cherish and to better serve the American people. My Administration is focused on promoting freedom and opportunity so that our Nation continues to thrive. As a result, a renewed sense of optimism is spreading through cities and towns across our great country.

Thank you again for your support. I am confident that together we will continue to build a stronger and more prosperous Nation for all Americans.

Sincerely,

Enclosure #2

Search for
Legal
Representatives
Law Firms

Dear Sir/Madam:

Does the Legal Profession have an association of legal firms? If yes, there is a dire need to open a new area of desperately needed legal representation for participants of the CIA's Artificial Intelligence Experiment?

At nearly 80 years, I will soon be enable to act as and advocate for my son who has been living with me since April 2016. I invited him to live with me because of suspected abuse of my son by the CIA for three prior years when he was living alone in his apartment. He was persuaded to leave his apartment and live in the hotels/motels because he faced some sort of external threat. After leaving his apartment he was encouraged to sell his car probably for the purpose of making him less independent and more vulnerable to CIA direction and Black Ops.

During the first years, of a current total of seven, I saw my highly intelligent and highly trained son with a MD degree as well as accomplished cancer research at the National Cancer Institute at Fort Detrick in Maryland. Subsequently I learned that he was directed by the CIA to terminate all friendships including family contacts. The CIA has only tolerated my four-year involvement with my son without meaningful lengthy discussions. Further my son was not to use radio/TV furthering his required isolation.

The proof/evidence which could support my testimony is an MRI of son's body/brain which could show a microchip(s) and/or a receptor(s). I contemplated scheduling a MRI for him to include in my book to raise awareness of my son's loss of liberty, freedom, sleep deprivation and torture/tormenting. If I am correct regarding the presence of an MRI/receptor, I am concerned that with the skull directed microwaves by the CIA to the brain together with the technology provided by MRIs could result in a massive brain hemorrhage.

Certainly if my son is still in the service/enslavement of the CIA at the time of my son's passing a brain scan/MRI will be made to determine the result of years of 24/7 voice to skull technology. Therefore, any book deal for my manuscript lacks the evidence that Michael F. Bell's <u>The Invisible Crime</u> provides.

Barring a Presidential Pardon/Gracious Dismissal, my only hope of effectively advocating for my son, who may soon be totally alone in the world, will leave my highly intelligent and cooperative son with the CIA all alone. He will be completely vulnerable to the CIA's Black Ops.

Is it possible for your firm and/or association of legal firms to find methods to defend victims of CIA's AI Experiment? It's possible many thousands of cases like my son's require sound legal defense which may require U.S. Supreme Court involvement?

Thank you for your consideration!

Enclosure #3

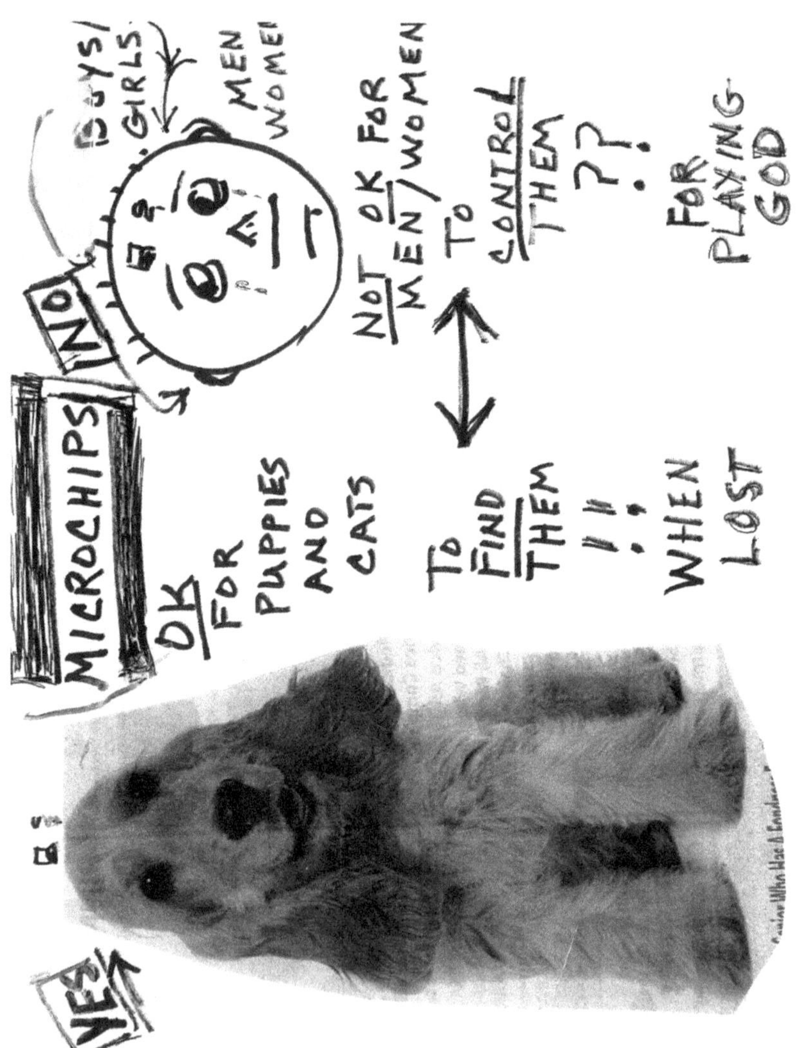

Microchips and/or receptor devices

ABOUT THE AUTHOR

As a father of a wonderful son, I was blessed by God to have a second chance to demonstrate my love for my son. I was challenged to find a way to free my son from his enslavement to high-tech embedded micro chip(s) and or receptors. A microwave machine is directed at home for 24/7 capability to brainwash my son's brain. An MRI was not done for fear of causing brain damage such as hemorrhaging, etc.